Make a Note to Love Your Spouse

A Step-by-Step Guide

for Making, Writing, and Delivering

REAL Love Notes

Jim Maxwell

Copyright © 2007 by Jim Maxwell

Make A Note To Love Your Spouse
by Jim Maxwell

Printed in the United States of America

ISBN 978-1-60266-366-4

All rights reserved solely by the author. The author guarantees all contents are original and do not infringe upon the legal rights of any other person or work. No part of this book may be reproduced in any form without the permission of the author. The views expressed in this book are not necessarily those of the publisher.

Unless otherwise indicated, Bible quotations are taken from New Living Translation of the Bible. Copyright © 2003 by Tyndale House Publishers, Inc.

www.xulonpress.com

Dedication

To Susan,
You are my
inspiration and reason
for REAL Love Notes

Contents

Dedication 3
Acknowledgements 6
Introduction 7
Chapter One: Why REAL Love Notes? 11
Chapter Two: What are REAL Love Notes? 19
Chapter Three: Principles of REAL Love Notes 23
Chapter Four: Getting Started 31
Chapter Five: Making REAL Love Notes 47
Chapter Six: Making the Message 67
Chapter Seven: Delivering the REAL Love Notes 73
Chapter Eight: Advanced Techniques 79
Chapter Nine: REAL Love Letters 89
Appendix I: REAL Acronym Possibilities 99
Appendix II: Occasions for REAL Love Notes 100
Appendix III: Recognitions and Celebrations 102
Appendix IV: Helpful Websites 107
Appendix V: Month and Anniversary Gift Information 108
Appendix VI: Favorites 110
Appendix VII: Recommended Reading 115

Acknowledgements

Thank you to Susan for your encouragement, inspiration, support, and technical help with the book and everything else. You do more than I can thank you for and I love you more than I can ever tell you no matter how many REAL Love Notes I give you. I'll keep giving them anyway.

Thank you to Tristan and Connor for putting up with Dad being on the computer instead of in the yard sometimes. Thanks to Lisa, my sister-in-law, for being excited about REAL Love Notes and believing they're a good idea. Because of all of you, this book is possible and better because of your support.

Introduction

This is a book about writing REAL love notes. Almost everyone appreciates getting a love note. A REAL love note in this book has a broad definition, and means a note from one person to another person for the purpose of making them laugh, encouraging that person, telling them you love them, or any other nice reason you can come up with to write a note. The primary audience is married people, followed closely by dating people. However, parents can use these same ideas with their children as well, and by extension, grandparents with grandchildren and vice versa. The list goes on and on.

REAL is an acronym for Romantic, Encouraging, Adaptable, Loving. It is part of the name of my business, REAL Marriage. You can get more information about marriage, preparing for marriage, marriage related topics, and even order REAL Love Notes at my website, www.myrealmarriage.com.

You also get to do your own defining of what a REAL marriage is since your marriage and my marriage will be different, and yet they can both be REAL. Take each letter and come up with some words that describe your REAL marriage, or words you would like to describe your REAL marriage. I am convinced that REAL Love Notes can help you have that REAL marriage. See the Appendix for a list of words to fit the REAL acronym and jumpstart your thinking.

I'm writing this book for a number of reasons. I think people specifically need help in writing love notes, and most of the guys I have contact with appreciate a few hints on how to score points with their wives. We are now heavily reliant on telephone contact, especially cell phones, and on e-mail, so I think people need a reminder of how to send messages in written form. Text messaging does not count as a written form, in my book, though I do think it is a good way to send loving messages.

Another reason is that reminders help us do what we used to do when we have forgotten or become too busy to remember what we used to do. It is a common cliché that once the marriage starts the romance ends. It is, unfortunately, often true. The notes, gifts, and dates that were once common become wistful memories.

Writing notes, especially REAL love notes, is fun. You had fun when you started dating, why not continue the fun? So this book is one of my contributions to making relationships and marriages better. And honestly, (honesty is one of the principles of writing REAL love notes) if I make a little money off of the endeavor then I can afford to send my wife some of the bigger or fancier notes I tell you about later in the book.

REAL love notes are loving, fun, caring, interesting, humorous, serious, and a host of other adjectives. REAL love notes also increase the love between you and those to whom you give them. While I concentrate on notes sent to spouses, the principles work well for sending notes to your children or other people you care about as well. Most of us won't turn down more love. Start sending those notes today.

In this book I'll tell you what I think a REAL love note is and all of the ins and outs of getting those notes to the people you want to have them. I'll tell you why you can send REAL love notes to people other than your family or your romantic interest. You'll learn some simple things that will make your notes special while not taking all of your time. For the more creative among you, I'll give you my ideas to make your notes more wanted than the newest toy at Christmas and more appreciated than expensive gifts. For the more well to do among you, I'll give you some ideas to help you spend that money on some expensive REAL love notes.

Throughout the book, I will put quotes in the book like the one you see below.

Somebody Said

"It's okay to use somebody else's words if they say what you want to say." — Jim Maxwell

For the purpose of illustration, I put in a quote from me. In the rest of the book, I'll put quotes about marriage, love, romance, or other interesting quotes to spark your thinking or to give you something you can put on one of your REAL love notes. A book of quotes can make your REAL love note writing easier and the Internet is a great resource for quotes.

Another item in the book will be tips to use in making, writing, and delivering your REAL love notes. These tips look like the one below.

> REAL love notes are good for any occasion.

REAL love notes are easy to do, they brighten the other person's day, increase love between you and the recipient, are fun to make and give, and pay big rewards. I would also like to think they will decrease divorce, affairs, cold families, and stress while increasing good marriages, good families, and a more peaceful world. So to have a good marriage, good family, and world peace— read on.

Why REAL love notes?
Chapter One

Why write REAL love notes? The number one reason to make and write REAL love notes is to let the person getting the note know you love them. Love is a broad term here, meaning anything from your general love of humankind and not wishing bad on anyone, to the love you have for your spouse. With all of these levels, it means we can send notes to the mail carrier, co-workers, our children, our spouse, and just about anyone else. It is okay to love people and let them know it. When you take the time to give or send a note, it says you care. After all, you had to put effort into the note and that also means time. It may not have been much time, but it was time **you** spent caring about the person who receives your note.

> *Somebody Said:* Love is above all else, the gift of oneself. — Jean Anouilh, Ardèle ou la Marguerite, Act II

One of the key ways most of us determine whether or not we are important to someone is to think about how much time that person spends with us. If someone tells you that you are important to him or her, and yet that person spends very little time with you, then you usually start to think you really are not all that important to the person. Yet a phone call, a note, or a short visit from that person can turn things around. The more frequent the better.

> Most REAL love notes can be made in less than sixty seconds. Everyone can invest at least sixty seconds in their marriage each day.

The number two reason for making and writing REAL love notes is to make deposits in your loved one's love bank. Everyone has a love bank and the bigger our account, the better. Other reasons for making and writing REAL love notes are to be goofy, be encouraging, be sympathetic, pick up a person's day, wish a happy birthday, celebrate a promotion, and a gazillion other ideas or reasons.

So, which is better, one really great note or letter a year, or a caring note two or three times a week, or a brief note daily? Well, it is kind of like advertising. Have you noticed how often you see advertisements for products? How likely are you to buy a product if you see the advertisement only once? Probably not very likely, which is why you are constantly bombarded by advertisements even from well-established brands? And all of that advertising must work or the companies would not continue to invest millions of dollars of their budget in doing it. The companies with the best advertising usually have the best sales.

> *Somebody Said*
>
> Doing business without advertising is like winking at a girl in the dark: you know what you are doing, but nobody else does. — Ed Howe

In essence, you are advertising yourself to the one you love and whose love you desire. Do you want to advertise only once a year, or do you want to "sell" yourself to your loved one by constantly bombarding them with advertising? REAL love notes are part of that advertising. You need to have better advertising than the next person, or you may find yourself replaced with a new brand. Of course, once you have sold yourself, the product needs to deliver.

> To "sell" yourself using REAL love notes make the notes about your loved one. For example, make the message, "You're cute!"

John Gottman is a marriage researcher and therapist. In his book, *Why Marriages Succeed or Fail*, he says that marriages where the positive outweighs the negative by a ratio of five to one are more likely to succeed. REAL love notes are one way to increase that positive ratio.

Another marriage therapist, Willard Harley, talks about the importance of meeting emotional needs and about the love bank, in his book, *His Needs, Her Needs*. He says every person needs to have their emotional needs met. This is not so hard to believe.

He also says that every person has a "love bank". Think of the "love bank" as a bank account where you make deposits and withdrawals. The basic idea is that when you do something your loved one, or the person you are interacting with, thinks is nice, then it is a deposit. The more deposits, the more love. When you do something the other person thinks is negative, it's a withdrawal. The more withdrawals you make, the less love you have in your account with that person. The way to be rich in love is to make plenty of deposits and few withdrawals. REAL love notes are deposits.

> *Somebody Said*
> In love and friendship, small, steady payments on a gold basis are better than immense promissory notes. — Henry Van Dyke

Every relationship has hard times. You keep money in the bank to pay for hard times that come, such as a broken transmission or busted water heater. You need to do the same thing for your relationship. REAL love notes are the constant addition to the love bank that builds a reserve for getting through the tough times. Sometimes, we do less than loving things in our relationships. The more we have deposited in our loved one's love bank, the more likely that person will work through the issue or event with us. Not only that, but the more you have invested in your loved one's love bank, the more likely you will avoid doing unloving things and you will want to make right what you have done wrong. The more you have invested in this relationship the harder you will work to keep the relationship and make it good.

How can a little piece of paper make a difference you ask? It is like compound interest. You know how this works in your bank account. You put money in your account and it gains interest. This means you have more money in your account and with compound interest you get interest on **all** of the money in your account, not just the original amount you put in the account. If you start with a small amount of money and you make only small deposits, it will take some time before you notice a difference. Yet, at some point that thing really takes off.

Somebody Said

A penny saved is a penny plus interest earned.

Unknown

There is another illustration that may be helpful in understanding the importance of regular REAL love notes. If I offer you $1000 a day for thirty days (which I am **not** doing, so don't write me for your money, it's only an illustration) or a penny today and I will double your money every day for thirty days, which would you choose? Many of you out there are saying, "Show me the money! Fork over my thirty grand so I can go on vacation." Others are saying, "There must be a trick here so give me the penny and double it every day."

For those of you who have heard it before, be patient with those who have not. Well, there is no trick here, just math. If you took the grand a day you have $30,000. If you took the penny doubled each day for thirty days you have $5,348,229.12 and a thirty one day month would give you over ten million dollars. Congratulations! You would be a millionaire. Sending REAL love notes on a regular basis will make you a millionaire in your loved one's love bank.

"What! That can't be right," you say. Yet it is. See the table below.

Day	Pennies	Money	Day	Pennies	Money
1	1	1¢	17	65,536	$655.36
2	2	2¢	18	131,072	$1,310.72
3	4	4¢	19	261,144	$2,611.44
4	8	8¢	20	522,288	$5,222.88
5	16	16¢	21	1,044,576	$10,445.76
6	32	32¢	22	2,089,152	$20,891.52
7	64	64¢	23	4,178,304	$41,783.04
8	128	$1.28	24	8,356,608	$83,566.08
9	256	$2.56	25	16,713,216	$167,132.16
10	512	$5.12	26	33,426,432	$334,264.32
11	1024	$10.24	27	66,852,864	$668,528.64
12	2048	$20.48	28	133,705,728	$1,337,057.28
13	4096	$40.96	29	267,411,456	$2,674,114.56
14	8192	$81.92	30	534,822,912	$5,348,229.12
15	16,384	$163.84	31	1,069,645,824	$10,696,458.24
16	32,768	$327.69			

Go ahead, check my math. Amazing isn't it? You can do something similar with REAL love notes.

Draw a picture of a piggy bank (or use a sticker) on the front of a REAL love note and on the inside write, "Here is my daily love deposit."

This is why I believe REAL love notes are important. Send one every day and see what happens. How quickly you see results and what kind of results depends on where you currently are in your relationship and the amount you have in your loved one's love bank. If you already have a big account then you will likely notice results right away and your account will grow even bigger. If you have a small account or are bankrupt then it will take longer to see positive results. Keep at it!

You can spend time pre-making notes once a week and add the messages later to fit the circumstances. You can also buy pre-made REAL love notes at www.myrealmarriage.com.

"How can I send a note every day? I can't think of that much mushy stuff to say." The beauty is you don't have to think of all that mushy stuff. Read on and I will take you through the process of making and writing REAL love notes. It really is simple and a ton of fun. And it pays really big dividends.

Use this space to take notes or write down REAL Love note ideas.

What Are REAL Love Notes?
Chapter Two

Part of good relationships is good communication and part of good communication is clear understandable communication. This chapter is an example of clear understandable communication. I want to make sure you understand what a REAL love note is, so that you have no trouble writing REAL love notes.

Simply put, a REAL love note is a written communication to a loved one to let that person know you care. Later on, we will expand that definition to include some other things but this is the basic idea.

Somebody Said

Married couples who love each other tell each other a thousand things without talking.

Chinese Proverb

"That sounds pretty broad," you say. Yup. People need to know you care and that you love them and that can be done, or said, in a gazillion ways. In a future chapter, we will look at developing messages, but I want you to see that a love note can be a "sticky note" with a smiley face drawn on it. While that may not be poetry or even a good movie line, it is love. "I can do that!," you say. Yup. That's my point.

Begin a file folder or notebook where you can put ideas you have for REAL love notes so that anytime you need an idea for a REAL love note you have ideas waiting. Out of ideas? Click on the "REAL Love Notes Tips" category at www.myrealmarriage.com/blog.

The main idea was expressed in Chapter One (you did highlight or underline that right?). Letting that special someone know that you love them is the main idea. It is nice to find a smiley face note made for you. How about a, "Have a nice day"? "Thinking of you" and "I love you," are also loving caring notes to give or receive. They can fit on very small pieces of paper, which you then give to the ones you love.

Somebody Said — If you love somebody, tell them.— Rod McKuen

This is a short chapter on purpose. I want you to understand that love notes are simple and easy. That may sound redundant, yet what you need to know is that making and giving a love note is not complex (so it is simple) and it is easy (so it does not take much time, supplies, thought, or money). This is because I want you to get started immediately. As you read through the book, you'll learn that it can be more complex (only if you want) and can take some time, supplies, thought, and money but again, only if you want. The more I play with these notes, the more fun I have.

So now I am going to help you with your first REAL love note. Later, you will do it all on your own but for now we will crawl. Later, we'll walk and then you'll take off running with your own ideas.

Get a pen and a piece of paper. Yes, do it right now. Fold the piece of paper in half. Write the name of the person you are giving the REAL love note to on the front of the piece of paper. On the inside write, "Have a great day!" Sign it, "Love," and your name. Now put your REAL love note where that person will find it. You've just written your first REAL love note. Feels good doesn't it?

Get up before your spouse and tape this note to his/her mirror to greet him/her in the morning.

Use this space to take notes or write down REAL Love note ideas.

Principles Of REAL Love Notes
Chapter Three

Really, I mean it— write that love note I told you to write in Chapter Two. If you already have, then write another one. You can even write the same note and put it in a different place. Now you've written at least one REAL love note. Keep up those deposits.

> Put this new note on his/her pillow.

Now that you have started writing REAL love notes, let's look at some principles for writing REAL love notes. These are guidelines or ideas to help you in the love note writing and making process. Think of them as a starting point and feel free to expand with your own ideas.

Principle 1 – Write REAL love notes

You have already been introduced to (and hopefully followed) the first principle, which is to write love notes. I really don't accept excuses here. It doesn't take much so write the note!

Somebody Said: Love is a verb. — Sister Mary Tricky

Principle 2 – Write and give REAL love notes frequently

Remember, you're making deposits in your loved one's love bank. The more deposits, the richer you are. While there are varying speeds at which your "wealth" will grow, I am confident that it will grow. Remember the doubled pennies. I suggest that the minimum frequency is once a week. By the way, this means that the loved one actually receives one love note a week. Later on, as you get into creatively hiding notes, it may take some time for your notes to be found.

As you discover the fun and benefits of making and writing love notes you will probably do it more often naturally. My REAL suggestion is that you average at least one note a day that you make and give.

Do so in a way that the loved one receives at least three notes a week. It will be fun for them (and you) when they eventually find the other notes. Currently, the longest it has taken my wife to find a note that I have placed for her to find is about a month. She liked it and I got credit for something I had forgotten I had done. That's a win-win situation.

Principle 3 – Be you

The person you are sending love notes to loves you because you are you so be you. Don't be me, Shakespeare, or some movie star. Be you. Use words you normally use. If you are going to use someone else's words then be up front about it. Tell your loved one that you really like the way this person said whatever it is you are writing and, you wanted to share it.

> You can score points by using the words of others that you know your wife likes. For example, if she reads the poetry of Emily Brontë then pick a line from one of her poems.

Principle 4 – Be real and honest

This principle is closely aligned with number three. Say what you really feel and use your own language. "I love you" is a powerful statement and meaningful to most people in the world. If you want to say it stronger and you want to use the "How do I love thee, let me count the ways" poem, then tell your loved one, "'I love you' doesn't really get the message across, but this poem does so I'm giving it to you." In this way the poem becomes your own language. More on this later.

Principle 5 – Use any reason

Use any reason you can find or make up to make and write a REAL love note. Sometimes the reason is, "its Tuesday." Any reason will do. Make up reasons or use some that come readily to mind. There is more on this in a later chapter and be sure to use the resources in the Appendix.

Principle 6 – Use favorites

When making and giving notes, use your loved one's favorites and even your own favorites. For example, if your loved one's favorite color is red, write the note using a red ink pen, pencil, or crayon. Fill out Appendix VI in the back of the book and you'll have plenty of favorites to use.

Principle 7 – Use convenient items

Use items that make it easy for you to make your notes. Much of this is covered in later chapters, so for now remember that you do not have to work hard.

Use sticky pads so you can put a message anywhere. Use pre-made blank notes and fill in with a message. Buy pre-cut paper so all you have to do is fold it and put a message on it.

Use stickers of all types. There are some silly and fun ones available at teacher supply stores (most people still like to get a gold star) and the craft stores have some very nice stickers.

> You can put a gold star on the front of your note and write "You're a gold star wife" on the inside.

They also have "embellishments" and many of these are peel and stick.

Principle 8 – Plan to write REAL love notes

> *Somebody Said*: You don't have to plan to fail; all you have to do is fail to plan.

Set aside some time each week to write REAL love notes. By making a plan, you are sure to write those REAL love notes. You can prepare a whole week's worth of notes in under ten minutes.

Because it is also a planning time, look at your calendar and plan your notes accordingly. This means if a birthday is coming up then you want to have an appropriately themed, decorated, and messaged REAL love note for the birthday. Upcoming holidays are good themes for a REAL love note and so are the "proclaimed days" like "National Day to send a REAL love note." Yes, I made that up but I am thinking of suggesting it to my Congressperson or Senator.

Principle 9 – Be spontaneous

"Didn't you just tell me to plan my REAL love notes? Make up your mind," you say. "Why?" I say. I do think it is good to plan REAL love notes, and I also know that sometimes a good idea hits me and I need to make that REAL love note right away or at least write the idea down in detail so I can make it later. You don't have to wait until your planned REAL love note making time, you can make them anytime and it's even a good idea. This fits with principle one, write REAL love notes.

> Keep a pen and paper with you to write down ideas you get and then transfer that information to your REAL love notes file folder or notebook.

Summary

Principle 1 – Write REAL love notes

Principle 2 – Write and give REAL love notes frequently

Principle 3 – Be you

Principle 4 – Be real and honest

Principle 5 – Use any reason

Principle 6 – Use favorites

Principle 7 – Use convenient items

Principle 8 – Plan to write REAL love notes

Principle 9 – Be spontaneous

Use these principles for writing your REAL love notes and you will get results. Since I don't know the person you are writing REAL love notes to I can't guarantee what result you will get, positive or negative, but you will get a result.

Positive results are thank yous, smiles, hugs, kisses, or even more positive things. Negative results are frowns, derisive laughter, sarcasm, or worse.

Do not despair if your result is negative. Pay attention to that negative result and it will give you information on how to better target the next REAL love note. Maybe you are trying this after some time of neglecting your loved one, so you are not considered sincere in your note writing. This probably means you need to continue to use the principles and wait for the deposits to get you out of the red in your loved one's love bank. You can do it!

> *Somebody Said:* When I was young I observed that nine out of every ten things I did were failures, so I did ten times more work. — Bernard Shaw

Use this space to take notes or write down REAL Love note ideas.

Getting Started

Chapter Four

Technically, you already started back in Chapter Two. Now I'm going to show you how to build on the piece of paper and writing utensil idea. By the way, go ahead and write another REAL love note right now. Try a sticky note (if you have one, if not, use another folded piece of paper) with the message, "I'm thinking of you" and sign it "Love" followed by your name. Stick this note on your refrigerator. Now you've made and given at least two REAL love notes. See how easy this is?

Somebody Said: Success in marriage is more than finding the right person: it is a matter of being the right person. Rabbi B. R. Brickner

Purchased Notes

Go to any number of stores and you can buy cards to give to people. Many of these cards come with messages so all you have to do is sign your name. Blank cards are nice because you can customize your message. Buying them from the store saves time in the creativity and production department. These are also handy to have around for sending nice notes when you do not have time or supplies for a more lengthy personal process. A nice card personalized by you can be just the thing.

When purchasing cards, I recommend that you buy a variety of types and sizes. Some will be small and some will be larger. Buy "fun" cards and "serious" cards. Buy cards that are "funky," "wacky," "silly," "intellectual," "romantic," "sexy," "meaningful," "humorous," etc. All of these adjectives can refer to the look of the card, the message of the card, or both. Cards that are blank on the inside are the most versatile.

Keep a small supply of notes at home, work, and in the car so you are always ready to give that REAL love note. File boxes for 3X5 cards work well as storage places and they protect your notes.

Paper

"Sticky notes" come in a variety of colors, sizes, shapes, styles, etc., and allow you to place your messages just about anywhere. You can branch out simply by varying which sticky pad you use. The heart shaped sticky notes are fun to have around and so are the star shaped ones. You can also get sticky notes in letter shapes, so get a pad of the first letter of your loved one's name and one of your name and stick those REAL love notes all over the place.

Paper also comes in a variety of colors, sizes, shapes, styles, etc. When it comes to making love notes, I primarily use card stock. It holds up better and it allows for things to be done to it, like punching, which you have a harder time doing to less sturdy paper types. No not with your fist, with a shape punch. But we cover this later.

Alliteration, the stringing together of similar sounds, for example, "plethora of places" or similar sounds, can be a fun thing to use in your messages.

Now that I have told you I primarily use card stock, I will also tell you that it is great to buy pads of specialty papers that come in a bunch of colors, prints, and textures. These are great for quick love notes. The ultimate quickness here is to tear off a sheet of this paper, fold it in half, and write a note on the inside.

For more advanced techniques, it is useful to have different types, textures, and weights of paper. These can be mixed on the same love note. It takes more time and tools, so we'll cover this in the chapter on advanced techniques.

Somebody Said

Duty makes us do things well, but love makes us do them beautifully. — Anonymous

Writing Utensils

How many things can you write with? I don't know for sure, but I do know that I like to use as many of them as I can. I suggest you do the same. The same words, on the same paper, in the same color can be different by using a different writing utensil. A note written in pen is different than a note written with a crayon and fat crayons write differently than skinny ones.

Below is a selection of writing utensils with some comments for each. Remember that most writing utensils also come in a variety of colors and the use of color is good. Color catches the eye, sends its own message, and touches the emotions. Color also adds variety.

Somebody Said

There are colors which cause each other to shine brilliantly, which form a couple, which complete each other like man and woman.
Vincent van Gogh

Dip Pens

I couldn't come up with a better name for this group of writing utensils. I use this category to refer to writing utensils with a hard tip that is dipped into ink or something else and then used to write. In my mind, this category includes quills (yes, you can still get them, no I do not have one) glass pens, "nib" or calligraphic type pens, and a stylus. Even though you don't have to dip them in the ink, I include refillable fountain pens and cartridge fountain pens in this category. You can find ink in a number of colors. Some of you may even figure out how to make your own ink and make it in whatever color you want.

Why use this type of writing utensil? There are two main reasons for using this type of utensil. The first is that sometimes the points on these utensils give you a different look because of the way they are made. All you have to do is write like you normally would and yet it looks different. Think of it as a manual way of doing bold or italics like you would on your computer.

The second reason is sometimes it is cool to write with one of these utensils. I like having a pen that I dip in ink and then write with and I typically use such a pen with parchment paper, which adds to the experience for me. It is okay for you to get enjoyment out of making the REAL love notes you send and it keeps you making and sending them.

Ink Pens

These pens come in all kinds of styles and ink colors. There are numerous tip sizes to ink pens so buy different sizes for different effects. Some use acid free ink (good for those notes you think the loved one will save, or for use in scrapbooking) others use gel ink, and then there is what I call standard ink. Take your pick.

Somebody Said

The palest ink is better than the best memory.

Chinese proverb

Markers

Markers come in an even wider variety of tip sizes than pens do so that you can make from very thin lines up to very fat lines. You can get colors to your heart's desire and again you can get acid free ink. There are a number of different types of tips to markers such as "chisel," "calligraphy," "brush," and "writer" to name a few.

While you may not want to learn calligraphy as a way of writing you can change the look of a REAL love note simply by using a marker with a "calligraphy" tip and writing like you always do. Markers also come in a variety of types such as "permanent," "erasable," "fabric," and "glass." These types of markers increase the number of mediums, or places, you can safely use to write REAL love notes.

Pencils

Pencils are like pens, only more easily erasable. Colors abound and they are easy to find. Pencils also work well for those quick notes where the only smooth solid surface to write on is something vertical. Don't forget "grease" pencils.

Crayons

Crayons come in what I call the regular size and the fat size. Both can be found easily. The regular ones come in at least 96 colors, and that does not include the specialty ones that are "glitter," "neon," or some other type developed to increase your creativity and lighten your wallet.

Before you paint your bedroom, use crayon or some other writing instrument to write REAL love notes to your wife all over the walls. Let her know that those words of love will always be there under the new paint, sending their message of love.

Pastels

This is the name I give to any color of small (about 3") rectangular type, almost crayon-like utensils found in the art section of stores. My wife calls them "creypas." The colors move beyond pastel into the full spectrum of colors and this utensil is different than a crayon.

Chalk

Yes, chalk. It can be used on paper, especially black paper (something else we will talk about later) and it comes in more colors than white. You probably already know about sidewalk chalk, which, by the way, is one more way to give a REAL love note.

Brushes

While we think brushes are used for paint only there are people, most quick to come to mind are the Chinese, who use brushes with ink for writing. Using a brush brings something different to your writing. Feel free to use ink or paint.

Decoration

Decorating your REAL love note adds a special flair and does not have to be difficult. You can decorate a REAL love note and write the message in less than sixty seconds. Really! You can take longer if you want, yet special touches can be done quickly. You can decorate the outside, the inside, the corners, and the edges of your REAL love notes. Let's look at some decorating ideas.

> *Somebody Said:* Every day should be distinguished by at least one particular act of love. — Johann Kaspar Lavater

Stickers

Stickers are used for decoration and often convey part of the message as well. They can be serious, fun, humorous, beautiful, silly, inexpensive, expensive, flat, or dimensional. Dimensional refers to stickers (or what I also call "embellishments") that are not the same thickness as a piece of paper. These things "stick out" from the note so that the note is no longer flat.

These dimensional "stickers" also come in different kinds like paper, plastic, felt, fake gemstone, and others. The point here is that you have a number of options in adding to your REAL love note without much effort. Peel and stick is fairly easy.

Put a smiley sticker on a REAL love note and on the inside write, "I'm happy to be stuck with you."

There are also "rub ons." They are not quite stickers, but close. These are pieces of paper with messages or pictures on them that you place on your REAL love note and then rub with a craft stick (popsicle stick for us older guys) or something similar to transfer the message to the note. It is kind of like an iron-on without the heat.

Stamps

I do not mean those things you put on letters. I'm talking about things like rubber stamps, although there are also sponge types. Stamps can be used simply by inking them on a stamp pad and stamping your note. Stamps can also become very creative and advanced. If you don't want to buy a bunch of stamp pads in differing colors, then use some of those markers to ink your stamp and then stamp your note. In that way, you can even use more than one color at a time on the same stamp. Stamps are a basic technique that can become very advanced.

Foamies (Foam shapes)

Foamies are available at your local craft store and often the big "mart" type places. These shapes are thicker than paper and thinner than cardboard. You can get them in shapes, numbers, letters, and in all kinds of themes. Foamies are easy to put on your REAL love note using double sided tape (the kind in a dispenser is easiest) or a glue stick. Some are peel-and-stick. Of course, they come in a variety of colors and sizes and you can get sheets of craft foam to make your own shapes or even use it like you do paper as the basic medium for your REAL love note.

Paper

Paper makes great decoration. Paper comes in many colors, finishes (smooth, textured, glossy, etc.), sizes, weights, and prints. Paper on top of paper is decorative and sometimes you can simply use a fancy printed paper as the base level of the note. Small leftover pieces of Christmas/birthday/gift wrap can be the basic note or added decorations. With a pair of scissors, you can get the size and shape you want or you can use a shape punch, which is easier.

Embellishments

I mentioned embellishments under stickers but not all embellishments are peel and stick.

> Glue a cotton ball to the front of a note and write, "I've really taken a cotton to you."

It is amazing what you can find at the craft store to embellish your REAL love note. I mentioned fake gemstones (the ones I bought were peel and stick) yet there are also embellishments made out of wood, plastic, felt, metal, and who knows what else. Some are shapes with words on them and some are just shapes.

Included in this category are brads. Brads come in many varieties, sizes, and colors. To use these, it is also helpful to have a push pin to make a starter hole in the note. Once you have made the hole, then push the brad through the hole and separate the pieces on the back like you do for those manila clasp envelopes.

Brads can also be your means of attaching other decorations to your REAL love note. My wife likes to take a paper shape, place it on the note and put the hole through both of them with the push pin and then attach it all together with a brad. She has even been able to match the paper shape with the brad shape (flower to flower or heart to heart) for a great decorative coordination.

Learn to use brads and match them to the note and your wife will brag on you to her friends, and possibly reward you in other ways also. Brads are easy to use and add a touch much greater than the effort needed to put them on your REAL love note.

Ribbon

Ribbon makes a good decoration for the edges of cards, or in decorative striping. You can also make bows and attach with hot glue or brads. Ribbon takes a little more work so I save it for nicer REAL love notes. You can often find ribbon on sale at craft stores or sewing type stores.

Before you dismiss the ribbon idea, remember a couple of key ideas. The first is that you are making the REAL love note for a loved one and if you are thinking about ribbon, it is for someone you really love like your spouse. The second thing to remember is that ribbon is for the special REAL love notes, so it is not a daily thing. Besides, decorating with ribbon probably adds one or two minutes. You can make a very special REAL love note in three minutes and make a huge deposit in the love bank.

Colored Glue

Did you know there was such a thing as colored glue? I grew up with plain old white for my glue and it worked just fine. Now, however, you can get glue in different colors. "Why bother when it will be covered by what you are gluing on the REAL love note?" you say. Because this is where you will be a little different and not cover the glue. Use it to make a design or something non-designed and let it dry. It will add color to the note and it also adds texture as it will dry "raised." It is fun and ladies like it when you get creative this way. Need I say more?

Somebody Said Love is being stupid together. — Paul Valéry

Photos

Put a photograph on the front of your REAL love note or on the inside. You can always "crop" (cut to size or shape or both) a photo to use in or on your note. With digital cameras, it is now easy to manipulate photos to make them smaller or bigger or to print them on various papers. Another thing to do is to print your photograph as a "watermark," which means it becomes a background on your paper. Noticeable but faint, and you can often choose how faint or not and then write on top of the photo. Be creative and reap the benefits.

You can now get printable stickers. Go to your office supply store to the section where computer labels are kept and look around. Take these blank stickers home and print out pictures or REAL love notes and stick in appropriate places.

Where do I get this stuff?

This is a good question. The answer is, "Just about anywhere." Your local grocery store may have basic items and so might the local drugstore. Wal-Mart, K-Mart, Target, and similar places have most of these basic items as well as some items for more advanced techniques.

Teacher supply stores are a good place to find stickers and some kinds of stamps. Gold stars and blue ribbons are useful in any number of messages and if you let yourself go a little bit, you'll find that you can use any number of items from such a store to send a bunch of loving messages in a bunch of ways.

Art supply stores have lots of items but usually are more expensive. Hobby shops also have useful items. There are now stores dedicated to scrapbooking and there are some companies, such as Creative Memories, that sell through parties at a person's home. If your wife or loved one is in to scrapbooking, then you may be able to find the number of a local representative or find it on the Internet. If you buy items for your loved one for use in scrapbooking, then you can use those items for making REAL love notes and you'll get additional deposits in the love bank.

My favorite place is craft supply stores, as you might have noticed me mentioning throughout. It is helpful to get things at these places because you can find all of these items at the same store. Card stock and paper are your primary resource and come in a number of sizes, colors, and textures.

Somebody Said Be prepared. — Boy Scout Motto

Now Keep Going

You have already made and wrote a few REAL love notes and you see how easy it is. You have just read through a number of options and you don't need to use all of them to be successful. Take time right now to write another REAL love note. Get in the habit and your REAL love note writing will become easier and more fun. Turn the pages as I take you through the steps of making a REAL love note.

Somebody Said: Sow an act, and you reap a habit. Sow a habit, and you reap a character. Sow a character, and you reap a destiny. — Charles Reade

Use this space to take notes or write down REAL Love note ideas.

Making Love Notes

Chapter Five

Did you make that REAL love note from the last chapter? You did! Great! Give yourself a pat on the back. Oh, some of you didn't? Well, get a piece of paper and something to write with and write that note **NOW!**

Somebody Said: Procrastination is one of the most common and deadliest of diseases and its toll on success and happiness is heavy. — Wayne Gretzky

This chapter is about making the note part of the REAL love note. It is the physical part of the note that has the message on it. Sometimes, this part is quick as when leaving a note on your spouse's mirror, desk pad, or on a sticky note. In this case, there is more to think about in the message areas.

At other times, it can take more time as you choose colors, textures, whether or not to layer, and other items. Just remember, some notes may only take five seconds (yes, it can be that quick) and others may take fifteen minutes (though this is rare), but most can be done in under two minutes.

> Putting something only the two of you understand on a REAL love note is a quick way to do a meaningful note.

For this chapter and the next two chapters, it is important to remember the five "W's." These are who, what, when, where, and why. It is also good to throw in an "H," for how. These organizational steps will help you make and write REAL love notes that are fun and meaningful for both you and the recipient. Once you learn to go through the five "W's" and an "H," then making and writing REAL love notes will be so easy that you will wonder why you haven't done it all your life.

Step One: Answer the five "W's" and an "H"
Who

Who is the note going to? Answering this question can help you make some choices. If the note is going to your wife and her favorite color is yellow, then yellow cardstock or paper can be a good choice. If the note is going to a co-worker or client (thank you notes are a loving thing to do and general love for your fellow human beings is acceptable), then the message is different than the message to your wife.

Somebody Said: Good manners are made up of petty sacrifices.
Ralph Waldo Emerson

Anyone is an appropriate person to send a REAL love note to. A birthday card is considered a REAL love note. Most people like to be remembered on their birthday even if they say otherwise. A handmade REAL love note not only lets the person know you remembered it also lets them know you care. Birthday REAL love notes are great ways to stay in touch with people.

The notes you send those you see regularly will be different than the notes you send to people you see once a year or once a decade, and yet they are all important.

What

What is the reason or occasion for giving this person a note? Though your wife's favorite color is yellow, if she is battling an illness that includes nausea, you might want to send a "get well" love note on green paper. Be sure that your humor will be well received, otherwise play it safe. Likewise, if she just received a raise at work, you can send a congratulatory note on green paper. This overlaps with the message itself and is covered more in the chapter on "Making the Message." See the appendix for lists of reasons and occasions to help you answer this question. Just remember, any "what," or reason is a good reason to send a REAL love note, just make sure the message fits the "what."

Somebody Said

Kind words are like honey – sweet to the soul and healthy for the body.—Proverbs 16:24 NLT

When

The "when" has more to do with delivery than with the making though they do go together. If the "when" is "immediately," then any noticeable size will do, but if the "when" is when she next opens her flip phone then the size has to be small enough to fit in the phone unseen.

"When" also becomes important if there is a particular "what." For instance, if sending the above birthday REAL love note, it is a good idea to get it to the person on their birthday or a little earlier is okay if mailing it. Those Christmas REAL love notes need to arrive in December before the 25th, but not in July, unless of course, this is part of a humorous interplay between you and the recipient, then mix up holidays all you want. I personally think it is okay to celebrate Valentine's Day on the 14th of every month, to celebrate birthdays each month, and to celebrate anniversaries each month. It's hard to have too much joy.

Be sure to give a REAL love note each month on your anniversary date, her birthday, and the 14th for Valentines Day as a minimum. Add in a REAL love note on the birthday of each of your children and send the children a REAL birthday note each month as well.

Another thing to remember is the difference between public and private notes. "Have a nice day" notes are okay to receive in public. Other notes may only be good for private viewing. You really don't want a private note to be seen in public because then it becomes a withdrawal instead of a deposit.

Where

The "where" is closely related to the "when." "Where" has quite a bit to do with delivery of your note so make sure to read Chapter Seven. If you have put the note in her flip phone then you know where it is, but you don't know where she will be when she opens the phone. Of course, you can call her to get her to open the phone and get the note and thereby influence where she receives it as well.

When hiding REAL love notes in shoes, make sure they are large notes on heavy paper so they will catch your spouse's attention. My wife and I have both walked around all day on REAL love notes left by the other in our shoes.

Chapter Seven has a larger list of "where" places to put the note but here are a few to get you started. Put notes in drawers, the medicine cabinet, in mittens, in socks, in the book your loved one is reading, on the car dash, or a million other places. It is often good to relate the message to the where the note is placed. Leave a REAL love note on the stove that says, "I'm hot for you!" Get the idea? Please make sure the stove is not on, or your spouse will be a different kind of "hot" when the house burns down. Always be careful that the placement of your note does not cause a hazard.

Why

The "why" is connected to the "what." Why are you sending the note? Is it a quick "hi" or another brief message? Maybe you are sending it to brighten a day or to celebrate a special occasion. For example, if you are sending it because it is Valentine's Day, then this influences color, shape, and decoration all before you even get to the written message. Whether or not you have been good or bad may also influence size, decoration, and content. I am reminded of a poster at my local florist showing three sizes of flower arrangements with the caption, "How mad is she?" This may apply to REAL love notes as well in size, shape, and numbers of notes you give.

Somebody Said: A perfect wife is one who doesn't expect a perfect husband. — Anonymous

How

The "how" is really about delivery. This includes timing and placement. Are you delivering the note in person or hiding it to be found? Are you having someone else deliver the note? Is it a paper note or is another medium involved, like a singing telegram. Check out Chapter Seven for more information on "how."

Step Two: Choose a medium

No, I do not mean someone to read your palm. Choose the medium, or surface, for your message. For now, let's stay with the basics, which are paper, cardstock, cardboard, dry erase boards, chalk boards, concrete, asphalt, wood, glass, mirrors, fabric, and metal surfaces like your fridge or a filing cabinet (if you have magnetic letters or words).

Each of these mediums influences what will be used to make the message. I do not recommend permanent markers on a dry erase board, mirror, or glass. I do not recommend paint on the sidewalk in front of your house, though sidewalk chalk is good here.

Almost anything that will leave a message is good on paper, cardstock, or cardboard.

You can even sew on paper and cardstock. Some specialty papers come with sewn designs and these are great for unique REAL love notes.

For your dry erase boards, please use only dry erase markers. You can tape a message made on another medium to the dry erase board. Chalkboards, of course, need chalk unless you are using a small one or old one that you want to leave a permanent message on, then paint or permanent marker works well also.

Concrete and asphalt can take chalk and pastels for areas that cannot be permanent and paint for areas where permanent is okay. Depending on the type of wood, most anything works, so have fun. On wood you can even use a wood burning pen or router, neither of which I recommend for other mediums.

Glass, mirrors, and metal will all take dry erase markers fairly well, or markers specifically made for glass. The metal surfaces will also take the magnetic words that are now popular in some books stores. You can use most anything on fabric and if you are accomplished at sewing or have a fancy machine, you can embroider your message.

Step Three: Choose a color

Choose a color for the medium you are going to use. Sometimes, you have no control over the color of the medium such as when you leave a note on the mirror. When using paper, cardstock, and fabric you have more choices than you might want. Keep in mind the favorite color of the person receiving the REAL love note and use it often.

Use your favorite color since, you will probably enjoy working with it and be more likely to make those REAL love notes. Keep in mind any colors that go with the holiday (red for Valentine's Day), special day (silver for that 25th wedding anniversary), or season (white for winter), at the time you are making your REAL love notes. Remember to use any colors that are easily associated with the message you intend to send.

Somebody Said: Color was not given to us in order that we imitate Nature. It was given to us so that we can express our emotions. — Henri Matisse

Color is important in that it sends a message all by itself. How you combine colors also sends a message. Some colors are complementary, whereas others—clash, and yet you can send a message either way. Make sure you're sending the message that you want to send. You can check the Internet for ideas and information about the meanings of color and uses of color. Here is some information about color that I have found.

Black

For you married guys, use black paper and write a message suggesting fun things you and your wife can do in the dark.

Black symbolizes grief and is associated with death, (the reason you see it at funerals) evil, and power. But it is also elegance, formality, night and mystery. Black goes well with bright colors. When using black paper it, is good to use silver or gold ink which can be quite classy. Black is a good color for writing your message since it shows up well on most other colors and black pens are easy to come by.

White

Use white paper to send an invitation to your wife to play in the snow.

White is the color of perfection, goodness, light, innocence and purity (which is why you see it at weddings). White also sends a message of coolness and cleanliness. It is easy to use and makes a good background for almost any other color. White is a good color to use for writing on dark-colored backgrounds.

Yellow

Send her a yellow note with the message "You are my sunshine," or send an e-mail with an embedded wav file of the song, "You Are My Sunshine." (Okay, you can stop singing now.)

Yellow is the color we use for sunshine. It represents joy, happiness and energy. It is a color for getting attention. Yellow is a good color for the medium of your REAL love notes, yet it does not do well as the color for writing unless you are able to outline it with another color. Yellow is a good color to use when layering your REAL love notes and yellow smiley face stickers are fun to use on REAL love notes.

Red

Cut out a bunch of paper hearts using red card stock, write "I love you" on them, and leave them in a trail from the front door to the bathroom where you have a bubble bath waiting for her.

Fire and blood are red, which makes this an intense color. It represents energy, danger, desire, passion, and love among other things. It is often associated with "stop." Red works as a background color or a writing color.

Pink

Send a REAL love note on pink paper that says, "Thinking of you tickles me pink."

Pink is considered a feminine color. It represents romance, love, and friendship. It makes a nice background color and depending on the shade, it can make a good writing color as well.

Orange

Send her a REAL love note on orange paper with the knock knock joke:
Knock, knock,   -   Who's there?
Orange,   -   Orange who?
Orange you glad we're together?

Orange is the color for fall, harvest, and pumpkins. It is a warm and energizing color. It represents joy, sunshine, and the tropics. This is another good background color and can work well as a writing color.

Blue

> On blue paper write the message, "You're cool!" and put it in the refrigerator for your spouse to find.

The sky and ocean are blue. It is a calming color and considered masculine. It represents heaven, faith, trust, loyalty, wisdom, intelligence, and confidence. Blue is a good background color and it is easy to find blue to write with as well.

Purple

> On purple paper, or with purple ink, give her a REAL love note with the words to the "Barney" song as the message.

Purple is the color of royalty. It represents power, nobility, luxury, and ambition. This is a good background color and works for writing on many colors. Purple is also a good color to use when layering your notes.

Green

On green paper, put a sticker of a traffic light, or draw one, and on the inside write, "Let's GO out tonight."

Green is the color of nature and represents freshness, fertility, growth, and harmony. It is associated with "go" and has healing properties, being the most restful color to the human eye (and my personal favorite). It makes a good background color or color for writing.

Step Four: Choose a texture

A REAL love note can go a long way in smoothing over a rough time.

Choosing a texture is mostly for paper, cardstock, and fabric. For example, I have smooth paper, bumpy paper, paper with patterns embossed on it, and paper that is stitched, to name a few. Each of these brings a different dynamic to the note you are making. Pick a texture that fits the message you are sending or enhances the message you are sending.

Step Five: Choose a size

Choose the size of the note you want to make. There are a number of factors to consider when choosing size. The length of your message may influence the size of your note. If you have a very long message, you may need more room to write it. However, you can put a very short message on a larger note. Depending on how small you write, you may be able to get a fairly long message in a small space. If you are sending the REAL love note then it needs to fit in an envelope.

Somebody Said: It's the little things that matter most: what good is a bathtub without a plug? — Unknown

Another factor is the placement of the note. If you are trying to hide the note in that special person's flip phone, then it needs to fit. If you are putting the note in a drawer, then you have greater size options. The size of your note may be part of the message and more will be said about that in the next chapter. Also, the supplies on hand may affect the size of your note. You may not have supplies to make the size note you want, so adjustment of the size or a trip to the store is necessary.

Step Six: Choose a shape

Somebody Said: A man is getting old when he starts to watch his own shape instead of hers. — Unknown

Notes can be done in an almost limitless number of shapes. Typically, we use a rectangle or square shape of some kind. It might be a small, medium, or large rectangle and yet this is where many of us get stuck. Be creative! Other shapes are fun and open up your options for the message and the delivery of the note.

Notes can be square, circular, oval, triangular, or anything else you learned in geometry. The rectangle, square, and triangle are the easiest to do. Others either take more skill or additional equipment. The other shapes are addressed in the chapter on advanced techniques.

Making a number of blank notes in a particular shape at once saves time. Spend a few minutes each week stocking up on different shapes and add the decoration and messages later.

Rectangle

The rectangle is the simplest shape to make since most paper and card stock comes in some standard sizes that are rectangular in shape. You make one fold on the paper and voila, you have a rectangular note half the size of the original piece of paper.

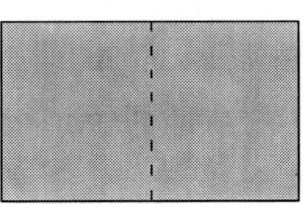

Square

Some papers and card stocks also come pre-cut in a square shape. This works well if you do not want to fold the note. Otherwise, to get a square shape you typically have to cut a rectangular piece of paper so that when you fold it you arrive at a square shape.

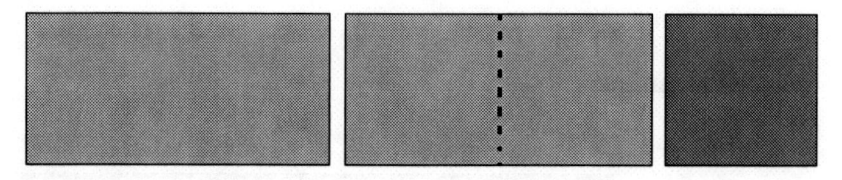

Triangle

The triangle note is easy to make. Take one of those precut square pieces of paper and fold one corner to the other corner diagonally and you have a triangle. Fold on the dotted line in the illustration below.

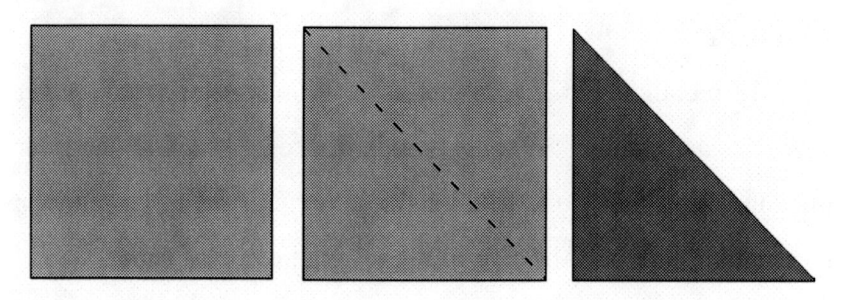

For a triangle that opens differently, start with a square piece of paper. Cut the square diagonally from one corner to another. Cuts like these are easier if you have a paper cutter. Now you have two triangles, which may be used for a non-folded note. You may also take one of these triangles and fold one corner to another to make a smaller size triangle that opens differently than the triangle made from a square.

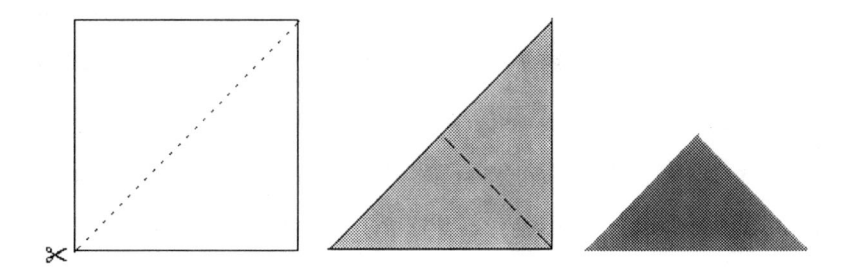

Step Seven: Choose an orientation

This step is also part of the message so I'll mention it again in the next chapter. This refers to which way the note opens and is read. For those familiar with how you print in common word processing programs, I'm talking about "portrait," which is the orientation of this book, and "landscape." "Portrait" means it is longer north and south than it is east and west. "Landscape" means it is longer east and west than it is north and south.

Somebody Said: How you see a matter depends on how you look at it. — Jim Maxwell

Another part of the orientation has to do with how you write the message, which can determine where you fold the note. I'll say more about this in the next chapter.

Step Eight: Choose your decoration

I am not a professional artist and I have not taken an art class since elementary school so realize that the following descriptions are not necessarily how an artist would describe them and some terms may be misused. You'll get the idea anyway.

Part of the decoration was taken care of when you chose the medium, the color, the texture, and the shape of the note. So what are you going to do with it now?

Stickers

> Give her enough REAL love notes and she will stop telling you where to stick 'em.

Stickers are probably the easiest decoration, just peel and stick. Stickers come in a multitude of shapes, sizes, colors, qualities, and types. Some stickers are humorous, some serious, some feminine, some masculine, some very flat and some with texture and depth. Peruse your local craft stores and you will find just about anything you are looking for in the way of stickers, and you will probably be surprised at the things that now come in sticker or peel and stick format.

Drawing

You may draw shapes, lines, pictures or whatever as decoration. This is where you get to use all kinds of writing implements. Remember that it is the thought that counts so don't worry about your abilities. Stick figures and other simple pictures work just fine. My wife says stick figures are a hit with women because it makes them look skinny.

Layering

Double sided tape in a dispenser is my favorite way of attaching paper to paper in note making. It is easy to use, quick, and you can find it just about anywhere you can buy tape.

You may use additional pieces of paper to decorate your note. A smaller rectangle, circle, square, triangle, or other shape may be taped (use double sided tape) or glued (glue sticks work well) to create a layered effect. You can use multiple shapes and offset layer them for a different effect.

Stamping

Stamping is easy. Take your rubber or sponge stamp, press it on a stamp pad, press it on your note and you're done. There are entire stores devoted to stamping, and these places will even teach you how to use them creatively. I'll address more advanced stamping in the chapter on advanced techniques.

Edges

Typically, when we fold paper (or the towels at home) we fold one edge completely to the other edge so that everything lines up neatly. That is not necessary when making REAL love notes. An offset edge gives the note a different look, and as we'll see in the next chapter, can be part of the message. Also, the edges can become part of the decoration, which we'll talk about in the advanced techniques chapter.

Photos

Photos are becoming easier and easier to use since the advent of the digital camera. Now, with a digital camera and a computer, you can put photos just about anywhere. You can also crop them or add text fairly easily, and resizing is a breeze. One idea for the use of your photos (thanks to my dear wife) is to use your photo as a signature instead of writing your name. This is a great idea for sending notes to younger children who may not be able to read yet.

Use a photo of the two of you on a date or vacation as a "watermark" for the inside of your REAL love note and tell her how much you enjoyed being with her.

Making The Message

Chapter Six

This the last chapter focused on the physical making of the note. Now that you have the physical note prepared, it is time to put the message on the note.

You may have already started the message in your making of the note. For example, in step one of the last chapter you answered the "five W's and an H." So if your spouse's favorite color is yellow, then you may be using yellow cardstock. This may add to the message the idea that you care about what your spouse likes. It may also be an, "I want to brighten your day," message and so the yellow color adds to the message. You get the idea. Decorate with a hand drawn smiley face and you have more of the message.

While this book presents making and writing REAL love notes in a linear manner, the actual making and writing of REAL love notes is not a linear process all of the time. Sometimes you come up with a message and design a note to put it on. Other times, you play with the physical note and then later add a message. Do what works for you and I'm sure your spouse will enjoy your REAL love note.

The medium may be part of the message as well. The medium is helpful in using a pun, or play on words, as the message. For example, you could write on a piece of wood, "Wood you go out with me Friday night?" Another example is to write on the lid of a can of peanuts (or whatever your loved one's favorite nut, besides you, is), "I'm nuts about you!" Don't let this backfire on you though by sending a message that is really only two-thirds of a pun—"P.U."

Color has already been addressed somewhat, so only a few suggestions here. Coordinating the colors of layers that you put on the note is fun and you can color coordinate with the color ink used in writing. A "missing you" love note can be on blue paper with the message "I'm blue without you☹." While color is important, don't forget that black and white are also colors and you can do great things with them. Just remember that when using black, or any other very dark color of paper, that you will need a writing utensil that shows up well on the note and yellow typically won't work. Silver and gold "gel" pens are my favorites for these dark colored papers.

Somebody Said Duty makes us do things well, but love makes us do them beautifully. — Anonymous

How often will texture make a difference in your note? My guess is that when it does it will usually do so visually. By that, I mean that the texture will do something to the medium that catches the eye and that may be the primary way it affects the message of your note. For instance, paper embossed with flowers will let you say something about flowers or to "give" flowers without giving a plant. It might be possible to have "bumpy" paper and talk about the "goose bumps" you got the last time the two of you kissed. Be creative and use all parts of the REAL love note to make your message. Putting in the thought and effort will mean as much as the REAL love note.

The size of your love note can contribute to the message. You can be very caring by putting a small "feel better soon" love note in your loved one's headache medicine bottle. You can get your message across by writing your "I love you in a big way" message on a refrigerator box. Size also has to do with delivery, as in the medicine bottle, but more about that in the next chapter.

The shape of the love note may or may not contribute to the message. A rectangular "I love you" love note is a good message. "I love you" also is a good message on a heart shaped piece of paper. If you have bought her a diamond ring, then a diamond shaped love note saying, "For another one of these look in your sock drawer," (where you have placed the ring) is a good idea.

Add this note with the diamond gift, "Diamonds are not the only thing that lasts forever, so does my love for you."

When it comes to putting the message on the REAL love note, there are a few things to remember. The orientation of the message does not have to be "square" to the love note. Typically, in English, you start at the upper left corner and go straight across the paper toward the right edge, return, and continue until you reach the bottom. You can write on an angle, in a circle, upside down, or any other way you can imagine. Have fun with it! Also, the message does not have to be written, it might be a picture type of message.

I am confident that you have already figured out how the decoration can be part of the message of your love note. The sticker of a sun with a smiley face in it might be the outside decoration for a love note that reads, "You're the sunshine of my life." Corny or hokey? Maybe. Effective? Try it and find out.

> *Somebody Said* — Love doesn't make the world go round— Love is what makes the ride worthwhile. — Franklin P. Jones

Near the end of the last chapter, I mentioned that the edges of your love note do not always have to line up. This too can be part of the message. A rectangular love note folded with the edges offset in anyway would work for an inside message that reads, "Things aren't right when I'm not with you," for when you have to be away. Remember, REAL love notes are about expressing love and that can be done in fun and creative ways.

> *Somebody Said:* We don't stop having fun when we're old; we're old when we stop having fun. — Unknown

Speaking of fun and creative – the more fun you have with making REAL love notes, the more you are likely to do it and the more deposits in your loved one's love bank you are likely to receive. Don't worry that what you are doing is too crazy or corny. This is part of who you are and it is important to put who you are into the making of your REAL love notes. Believe it or not, it is these things that endear us to our loved ones so we might as well capitalize on it.

> *Somebody Said:* I love you not only for what you are, but for what I am when I am with you. — Anonymous

Use this space to take notes or write down REAL Love note ideas.

Delivering The Message

Chapter Seven

Delivering the message is the last part of making and writing love notes. The delivery can also be part of the message. When your loved one opens the refrigerator and receives a blue REAL love note that says, "You're cool!" then you are coordinating all aspects of the message, color, placement, and message. Delivery of the message has two main aspects, the timing and the placement.

Somebody Said: In love and friendship, small, steady payments on a gold basis are better than immense promissory notes. — Henry Van Dyke

Timing

There is an old saying, "Timing is everything." While this is often true it is not always true. When it comes to delivering your REAL love note you have two options, "immediate" and "later". The "later" may be a "specific later" or a "whenever later."

Immediate

Somebody Said: Make hay while the sun shines.
English Proverb

This is simple. Make the REAL love note and hand it immediately to your loved one. There is no worry here about whether or not the note is received at the right time since you give the note directly to your loved one exactly when you want it delivered.

Hidden for a specific later

Some love notes are hidden in a specific place to be found at a specific time. Some events happen regularly and are a good time for REAL love notes. For example, you hide a "feel better soon" REAL love note in the place where your wife keeps her feminine hygiene products, or a "hit a hole in one" love note in your loved one's golf bag where the golf balls are kept. You have a pretty good idea of when that note will be found. You can also make notes specific to the hiding place. When you do this, you may know when it will be found or you may put it there and it will be found at some point in the future but you don't know when. This moves us to the next section.

Hidden to be found whenever later

Some REAL love notes are made and then hidden to be found whenever. It is good to do some of these so that there are those unexpected REAL love notes popping up. These are general REAL love notes that can be found anytime or anywhere and the message is still meaningful.

Somebody Said

They err, who say that husbands can't be lovers.
Anne Finch

Special Circumstances

When you are traveling it changes the circumstances for making and delivering your REAL love notes. You can always make a bunch of REAL love notes in advance and hide them all over your home. Another option is to make some in advance, take them with you and send them in the mail. Yet another option is to enlist the help of relatives or your loved one's friends to hide REAL love notes when they visit. You, of course, have made these REAL love notes and given them to the friends for placement while you are gone. Be sure to return the favor for them when they are gone. A special note here—leave the notes with a same sex friend of your loved one so that no one gets a wrong idea.

> *Somebody Said*
>
> A successful marriage requires falling in love many times, always with the same person.
> Mignon McLaughlin, The Second Neurotic's Notebook

These special circumstances apply especially to military personnel who are on long deployments. At the time of this writing, it is common for any military person in any branch to be on a deployment. Take your REAL love note making supplies with you if you can. This is more difficult for Navy personnel on ship but a few items may be possible. For other branches, you often are able to pack things in shipping containers, "MILVAN's," and have things when you arrive at your deployment. Put your REAL love note making supplies and a copy of this book in the container and keep up those deposits while on deployment.

A List of Hiding Places

The following is a list of hiding places and delivery options to get you started. Be creative and come up with your own or put a twist on these.

- Dresser drawers
- Inside clothes like socks, underwear, clothes pockets, jacket pockets, etc.
- Inside the pillow case
- Folded over the hanger of hanging clothes
- Inside shoes
- Inside bathroom drawers
- Medicine cabinet
- In the toilet paper roll (unwind some toilet paper and put the note in then re-roll it)
- On or under the toilet lid
- On the bathroom (or any other) mirror
- On the bath or shower tile
- On windows
- Inside pill bottles
- Glasses or sunglasses cases

- Contact cases (use small circles)
- Flip phones or phone cases
- Taped to anything
- Magnet boards or other places magnets will work
- Brief cases
- Purses or bags
- Folders
- The book your loved one is reading or the books on the "to read" pile
- In CD cases
- Planners
- Refrigerator
- Freezer
- Cabinets
- Microwave
- Dishwasher
- Computer screen (text or picture screen saver)
- Mailbox
- Steering wheel
- Sun visor
- Vehicle console
- Favorite coffee cup
- Tool box
- Sewing box
- Craft area

- Lunch box
- Lamp shade

Now that you have some ideas of where to hide those REAL love notes, what are you waiting for? Go make and hide some REAL love notes.

Somebody Said

Marriages may be made in heaven, but man is responsible for the maintenance work.

Changing Times: from "Notes on these changing times"

Advanced Techniques

Chapter Eight

Now is the time we take everything from the past seven chapters and go a bit further. Make sure you understand why you are giving, and hopefully making REAL love notes. Know what a REAL love note is and the principles of making and giving them. Once you have mastered the basics of getting started and making notes, you can start getting fancy once in a while. Remember, you can always send a simple note. Other times call for a nicer or fancier note. However, once you start getting fancy, you don't *always* have to be fancy, you can go simple again. Mix it up; it is better for you and the person receiving the REAL love note when there is variety.

Keep your supplies in one place so that you can make a simple or fancy REAL love note as the mood strikes you. Having your supplies in one place also sparks new ideas as you see them again.

Advanced Techniques for Making the Love Note

Once you have the basics of making a REAL love note, it is time to add to the basics. All of the steps are integrated so the separation of steps earlier was to get across a basic idea. Now is the time to bring these steps together to create a unified whole. It is kind of like putting together an all-star team. Each individual is good by himself or herself, however, if you want the team to do really well they need to work together so that the whole becomes greater than the sum of its parts. Believe it or not, many of these notes will be saved. Years later when your children or grandchildren find them they will learn valuable lessons from your creation. Teach them well.

Step one is to answer the five W's and an H. In the advanced form, this means incorporating the answers to these into the making of the REAL love note, composition of the message, and the delivery so that all of these components work synergistically to create a very special REAL love note.

Somebody Said

You will find as you look back upon your life that the moments when you have really lived are the moments when you have done things in the spirit of love. — Henry Drummond

Step two is to choose a medium. In advanced love notes, the medium is a very purposeful choice that enhances the overall message and experience of the REAL love note. Now is the time to break out the fancy paper or cardstock. Try using linen paper or handmade paper. Pick quality materials and it will show in the REAL love note.

> Try asking your wife what kinds of mediums, colors, textures, decorations, etc. she likes receiving. Asking may save you time and effort.

Step three is to choose a color. In the advanced mode, we are talking about choosing colors and we want those colors to work in such a way as to enhance the message and experience of the REAL love note. For some of us, this is difficult either because we are color blind to a degree (shades of red and green for me, which is ironic since my wife's favorite color is red and mine is green) or because we do not have much training or experience in this area. Don't despair; you can get better with practice. Pay attention to the color combinations your loved one has around or expresses appreciation for, and copy those.

Remember to choose color on purpose. Favorite colors are important and so are colors that are specific to the occasion of the REAL love note. For example, I could make a REAL love note for my wife to enjoy the Packer game one weekend (she likes the Packers and so do I) and coordinate cardstock colors in green and yellow. I could cut out a paper football or use a football sticker. In this case, I could also use a wedge of cheese. A twenty-fifth wedding anniversary REAL love note could be on silver paper or use silver writing.

Complimentary colors and subtleties add a special dimension to your REAL love note and yet sometimes purposeful clashing works well too. The more you make REAL love notes, the more proficient you will become in all of these areas. Don't stress, have fun!

> *Somebody Said:* Love is what makes two people sit in the middle of a bench when there is plenty of room at both ends. — Anonymous

Step four is choosing a texture. Everything I said about color is true for texture as well. There are what I call "3-D" stickers and decorations. For me, this means there is dimension to the item and it does not lay completely flat on the note. An example is that you can tape or glue a bottle cap or a button on the REAL note. These things "stick out" from the note and add texture. There are also "sticky dots" or "sticky foam," which is double sided and allows you to "raise" whatever you are sticking on your REAL love note off of the surface. This adds dimension to the note and literally makes your decoration stand out. You do not have to have "3-D" texture to have an advanced or special REAL love note, but it is an option.

You can also combine materials to create texture. For example, your base layer may be a nice smooth piece of parchment type card stock to which you glue ribbon. This creates texture and decoration. See how these work together?

Other places to add texture to your love note are the corners and the edges. If you have a steady and artful hand, you can do wonders with just a pair of scissors. An easier way to add texture to your note and jazz it up a little is to invest in some scissors that will cut your edges in different patterns. There are large numbers of these types of scissors and the store will sell you as many as you want to buy, but a few that you like will serve well. However, if your loved one is in to scrapbooking, you may already have access to such scissors. If not you can buy the scissors as a gift for your loved one and then use them to make advanced love notes. This is a win-win situation.

Investing in some tools from the craft store will pay big dividends. I am convinced that a $25 to $100 investment like this will prevent larger amounts of money paid to a counselor.

The corners are the other place I mentioned to add texture. Simply "rounding" the corners makes for a nice look. Here, too, you can use the scissors mentioned above to create different looks for your corners. There are also "corner punches" that will give you a variety of effects. These all cost money so choose wisely unless you have money to spare. I highly recommend a "corner rounder" as it will get its money's worth in use.

Step five is choosing a size. The size of your REAL love note can be very tiny to very large. You science people out there may find a way to get a small message on a small medium that your special someone who is also a science person can read under a microscope. Others of you with money to spare may invest in billboards or skywriting. If you want to say, "I love you" in a big way, then use a BIG REAL love note.

Another big REAL love note is to take out a full page in the newspaper. You can go less expensive by choosing a local community paper or free distribution paper in your area. If you really want to do it in a big way take out the full page ad in USA TODAY.

Step six is choosing a shape. The rectangle, square, and triangle were covered in Chapter Five. Now we move on to the oval, circle, and fan shapes.

Oval

The oval usually requires a punch or a template. My hand is not steady enough to cut this shape free hand with scissors. There are also companies that make "oval cutters," which are usually plastic shapes with a blade guide and blade made for the cutter so that you can cut the shape. These are available from the person who does those in-home scrapbooking parties or often at your local craft store.

The oval is great for folding in half. This is a slightly different shape than we normally see so it adds variety. Once you have folded that oval in half, you can cut the finished product in half and have two REAL love notes in a unique shape. Just remember to do all of your cutting before you add the decoration and message. Unless, of course, having it all done and then cut in half fits with the idea you are using, then put it all together and cut it in half.

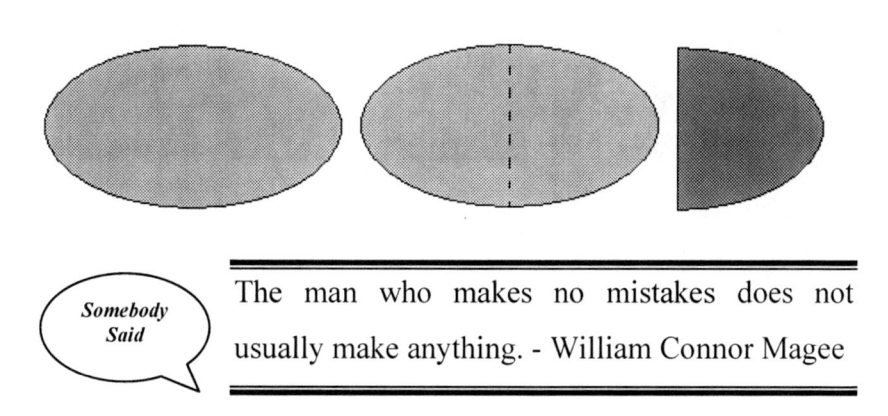

Somebody Said — The man who makes no mistakes does not usually make anything. - William Connor Magee

Circle

What I said about the oval is also true about the circle. You can get the same templates, punches, and "circle cutters" to do them in many sizes. Fold them in half or a quarter and have fun.

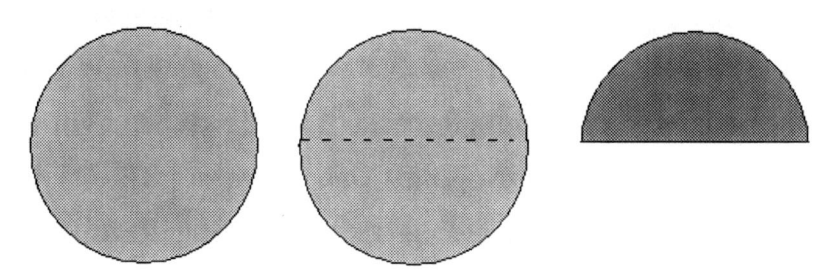

Fan

The fan is a shape I stumbled on thanks to my wife. I was working with the circle and folding it in half for a particular project and I discovered that I had cut too big a circle. The end result would not fit where I needed it to go. My creative wife took the folded circle to the paper cutter, placed the flat edge against the upper flat ruler of the cutter and cut the folded circle in half, which created what I call a fan shape.

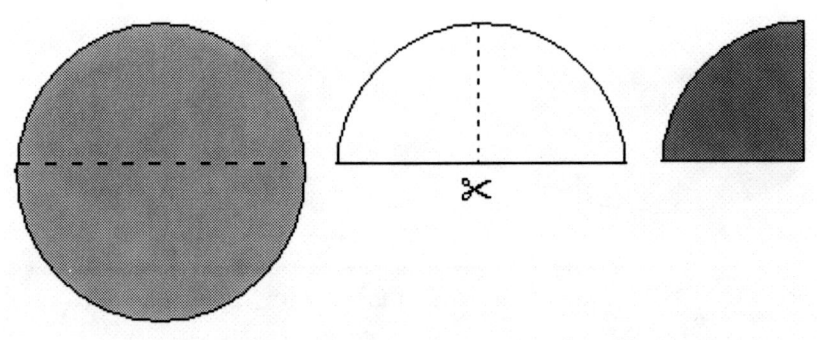

> *Somebody Said*
>
> Mistakes are the portals of discovery.
> James Joyce

The ideas are endless so be creative. Once you start making and giving REAL love notes, your creative juices will flow even more. In addition, once you are exchanging them with your special someone, you will probably adapt each other's ideas and continue to come up with new things for your REAL love notes. The key is to keep making and giving those REAL love notes.

There are times when we need to say more than we say on a REAL love note. Sometimes we need to write REAL love letters. There are many people in the military separated from their loved ones. E-mail and telephone calls are possible, yet there is something special about getting mail in the mailbox or at mail call. Sometimes we are just away on a conference for a few days. On these occasions, a REAL love letter says what a REAL love note does not have space to say.

Turn to the next chapter for some ideas on writing REAL love letters.

Use this space to take notes or write down REAL Love note ideas.

Love Letters

Chapter Nine

In a book about REAL love notes why write a chapter about REAL love letters? After all, who writes letters anymore? Don't most people pick up a phone or send an e-mail? Well, the why is because love letters are special, especially when they are REAL love letters. Many people do not write letters anymore because they can pick up a phone or send an e-mail and say immediately what they want to say. The problem is that phone conversations may be remembered and they may not. Some people save e-mails, yet many do not. A nice e-mail is, well, nice. A handwritten letter is special.

> *Somebody Said*
>
> Sir, more than kisses, letters mingle souls; for, thus friends absent speak. — John Donne

I believe there is a difference between a handwritten letter and one that is typed. I think it even engages the brain differently. A quick Internet search called up some research indicating that each person's handwriting is unique. That is not hard to believe yet it means that anything that **you** handwrite is unique. When you write a letter instead of typing it you give that person something special and unique. Add to that a few touches like special paper or color of paper or ink and you have given them something to keep in that special memories box. It is probably a deposit in the love bank as well.

> *Somebody Said*
>
> For God's sake, don't give up writing to me simply because I don't write to you.
> Robert Frost

So how do you write a REAL love letter? Start by using all of the principles listed in Chapter Three. As a quick reminder those are (as adapted for love letters):

1. Write love letters
2. Write and give love letters frequently
3. Be you
4. Be real and honest
5. Use any reason
6. Use favorites
7. Use convenient items
8. Plan to write REAL love letters
9. Be spontaneous

Once you have given thought to these principles for your love letter, then you can put them to use in a standard letter format. In the following pages there is a standard format with some explanations of each of the letter parts, along with tips on how to make your letter a REAL Love Letter.

Salutation (Greeting)

> Start your e-mails with a salutation when writing to loved ones. These people are still "dear" to you and the more they hear that (or see that) from you, the better.

This is the opening of the letter or the "Dear (insert name here)" part of the letter. Your REAL love letter may be serious, comical, plainly communicative ("This is what happened to me today and how I'm feeling") emotional, or any number of other adjectives. Use a salutation that fits what you want to say. For the REAL love letter expressing your deepest feelings of love, you might start with something like, "My dearest _____," or "My only true love." This is different from the REAL love letter that intends to be fun and cute which might start, "Dear Snugglemuffin." You get the idea.

Date

Always date your letters. The date puts the letter in the larger context of what is happening in the world and it keeps things straight chronologically. This is especially important for those who are away from their loved one(s) for an extended period of time and who are writing regularly. The United States Postal Service does a fantastic job of getting letters where they are supposed to go. That said, there are times when letters are delivered out of sequence if you are writing frequently from far away. There is probably any number of reasons for this, but this is a good reason to date your letters. When your loved one(s) receive your letter they can then put it into the proper order.

If you write more than one letter to the same person on the same day, be sure to number your letters. Unless you know you are going to write more than one letter, you probably won't number the first one. That's okay. Make sure to number everything after the first one that day and it will work out.

You may also want to include the time you write on your letters. A general time frame (morning, afternoon, evening) works. You can add an adverb for more specificity (early, mid, late) to come up with early morning, mid-afternoon, late night, or other combinations. Of course, you can always just put the time you start writing (4:32pm). If you are in another country, be sure to say if the time is local time for you or for the person receiving the letter.

> *Somebody Said*
> The love we have in our youth is superficial compared to the love that an old man has for his old wife. — Will Durant

Another reason for this dating and numbering is that it will help years later when the letters are looked at again. Most of us occasionally look through old letters, and having the date on them helps put them in perspective. Eventually, your children may see the letters and want to read them to understand you and your relationship better. Of course, you may end up being a famous person, in which case your letters are important as reference and historical documents. In either case, you are leaving a legacy for those who follow. They will understand better if they can put the writings into context by knowing when they were written. A side note: save the envelopes when you receive letters. The postmark adds to the information and can be cool depending on where the letter is postmarked.

Body

The body of your letter is the main area where you do your writing. Here is where you put the information you are sending and ask the questions you want to ask. Say to your loved one what you want to say. If you are writing what I'll call a "classic love letter" where you are waxing on about your love for your loved one then be descriptive and detailed.

Tell your loved one about your love with words that describe your emotion, your feelings. Also, write about your thoughts and the physical feelings or sensations that you are having as you write.

Somebody Said

How do I love thee? Let me count the ways. I love thee to the depth and breadth and height my soul can reach . . .

Elizabeth Barrett Browning, Sonnets from the Portuguese, #43.

If you are writing your letter because you love someone and are trying to stay in touch, you can use much of the advice about "classic love letters," only you won't be as mushy. Make sure to give details about your day or what is happening with you. Put down the "mundane" and "unimportant" stuff. It is these kinds of everyday things that enrich our lives when we share them with each other and it is these things that we miss when we are not with our loved ones. It's okay to tell about the big things too, just don't forget about the small things.

Make sure to use plenty of adjectives and adverbs. Remember your English classes? If not, check out some old episodes of School House Rock™. Adjectives describe things. A *blue* car, a *big* fish, a *happy* anniversary, etc. are examples using adjectives. Adverbs modify or explain verbs, adjectives, or other adverbs. A *dark* blue car, a *really* big fish, and a *very* happy anniversary, etc. are examples of adverbs. And yes, I had to check the dictionary to make sure I could tell you what adjectives and adverbs are and how they are used.

It is important to be descriptive enough that the person you are writing to "experiences" what you are experiencing. This sounds difficult to some of you and yet with some practice, it will become at least easier if not easy.

Somebody Said: O, my love's like a red red rose / That's newly sprung in June.
Robert Burns, "My Love is Like a Red Red Rose"

Closing

The closing is that saying that you write your signature under. In formal and business letters, it is often "sincerely" followed by a comma. It is proper to end your closing statement with a comma and then sign underneath.

The suggestions for the closing are really the same as the salutation. Use a closing that fits with the style of letter, the tone of the letter, and what you have said in the letter. Some closings you may want to think about are, "Love," "Yours Truly," "Forever yours," etc.

Signature

Do I really need to explain this part? Again, make your signature fit the letter and the person you are writing to. You can use your nickname (Jim instead of James), your birth name (James instead of Jim), a pet name (Snugglemuffin – and no, this is not a name used in our household) or whatever fits.

Love Letters to Children

All of the above suggestions fit for the letters you write to your children. In this case, you are leaving a legacy and it is important. Make sure to write the letter on your child's developmental level if you intend for the letters to be read by or to your children. There are some letters that you will send to, or put aside for, infants and young children and in these letters you can write what you need to write knowing the letters will be read when the children are much older.

Feel free to use crayon and draw pictures for the really young ones. It is also a good idea to include pictures you have taken along with a story about the picture.

Children like pictures and so do adults. Digital cameras make it easy to take plenty of pictures, which can be e-mailed or printed at the local photo processing place and then sent. Postcards are great and so are gifts from the area you are visiting.

Write to your children regularly. Write even when you are all at home. For those letters, you can put them to paper and mail them so the kiddos get mail, which they usually enjoy immensely, or you can buy a journal for each kiddo and write the letters to them in the journal. When they leave home to be on their own, you decide if going to college counts or you'll wait until they graduate and truly leave home, then give them all the journals of letters you have written. My suggestion is to do both of these. That way they get letters in the mail and they get something to take when they leave home.

About the journal letters: These are letters of things you notice about your children, things you want to say to them that you don't want to forget, things you want to say and they are not old enough to understand, or lessons you want to impart. These letters can be a blessing to your children throughout their lives.

Your children will appreciate these letters and journals. It's worth it to you and to them to write these letters.

> *Somebody Said*: Children have never been very good at listening to their elders, but they have never failed to imitate them. — James Baldwin

REAL love letters and REAL love notes are fun to make and write, great to give, and great to receive. Make and write REAL love notes and letters and give them to those you love. I truly believe it will enhance your relationship, increase your joy, and make the world a better place.

Use this space to take notes or write down REAL Love note ideas.

Appendix I
REAL Acronym Possiblities

"R" Words:
robust, racy, renewing, ready, radical, rapturous, rational, raucous, realistic, rewarding, reasonable, receptive, recharging, reciprocal, reconciling, recreational, recuperative, redeem, reflective, refreshing, regenerating, regular, rejoicing, rejuvenating, reliable, relational, relaxing, relevant, religious, remarkable, reminiscent, renovating, resilient, resourceful, respectful, restorative, rewarding, rich, rigorous, risqué, romantic,

"E" Words:
energetic, encouraging, enduring, energizing, eager, earnest, eccentric, eclectic, edgy, edifying, educational, effective, effervescent, effort, egalitarian, elastic, electric, electrifying, elegant, eloquent, embracing, empathic, empathetic, enchanting, engaging, enjoyable, enlightening, entertaining, enthralling, enthusiastic, enticing, equal, equipping, erotic, erudite, ecstatic, eternal, ethical, eventful, evolving, excellent, exceptional, exciting, exclusive, exemplary, exhilarating, exotic, exquisite

"A" Words:
abiding, able, absurd, accepting, accommodating, accompany, accomplished, accord, accountable, achievable, action, active, adaptable, adoring, adroit, adult, advantageous, adventuress, adventuresome, affirming, aggravating, agreeable, ailing, aimless, alert, alluring, altruistic, amazing, ambitious, amiable, amorous, ample, amusing, anchor, animated, apologetic, appreciative, appropriate, arousing, attainable, attractive, available, awesome, admirable, admire, admiring

"L" Words:

labor, large, laugh, laughter, legendary, limber, literate, lively, longsuffering, long lasting, loony, love, lovely, loving, loyal, luscious

Appendix II
Occasions for REAL Love Notes

Almost any reason is a good reason to send a REAL love note. Listed below are some occasions to keep in mind and give you inspiration for making and sending a REAL love note. I am giving dates where I can find them. Some of these days "float" and you'll have to check your yearly calendar or some of the websites listed in Appendix IV.

Weekly

"I love you"
"Have a Nice Day"
"Thinking of You"
A note related to whatever "official" week it is

Monthly

Their birthday
Your birthday
First date
Anniversary
A note related to whatever "official" month it is
Wife's menstrual cycle

Yearly

Each official holiday
Religious holidays
Made up holidays (e.g. National Talk Like a Pirate Day – September 19)
New Year's Eve and Day
Martin Luther King Jr's birthday (3rd Monday in January)
Benjamin Franklin's birthday (January 17)
John Hancock's birthday (National Handwriting Day-January 12)
National Freedom Day (February 1)

Groundhog Day (February 2)
Thomas Edison's birthday (February 11)
Valentine's Day (February 14)
Presidents' Day (3rd Monday in February)
Abraham Lincoln's birthday (February 12)
George Washington's birthday (February 22)
Mardi Gras
International Women's Day (March 8)
St. Patrick's Day (March 17)
April Fool's Day (April 1)
National Tartan Day (April 6)
Thomas Jefferson's Birthday (April 13)
Earth Day
National Arbor Day (Last Friday in April)
Administrative Professionals Day (Last Wednesday in April)
National Day of Prayer (1st Thursday in May)
Cinco de Mayo (May 5)
Mother's Day (2nd Sunday in May)
Memorial Day (Last Monday in May)
Armed Forces Day (3rd Saturday in May
Flag Day (June 14)
Father's Day (3rd Sunday in June)
Independence Day (July 4)
Poet's Day
Grandparents' Day (1st Sunday after Labor Day)
Labor Day (1st Monday in September)
Patriot Day (September 11)
Constitution Day (September 17)
Sweetest Day (3rd Saturday in October)
Columbus Day (2nd Monday in October)
National Boss Day (October 16)
Halloween (October 31)
Election Day (Tuesday following the 1st Monday in November)
Veterans' Day (November 11)
Thanksgiving (4th Thursday in November)
St Nick's Eve (December 5)
Christmas Eve and Day (December 24 & 25)

Appendix III
Recognitions and Celebrations

This is where you find out just some of the National Month/Week celebrations. I found these in a book or on a website so someone is celebrating them or recognizing them, which makes it okay for you to make and give a REAL love note. Check out the websites in Appendix IV for more information on these celebrations and to find more celebrations.

January
Hobby Month
Hot Tea Month
Prune Breakfast Month
International Creativity Month
National Get Organized Month

January by the Week
First Week – Diet Resolution Week
Second Week – Universal Letter Writing Week
Third Week – World Kiwanis Week
Fourth Week – National Handwriting Analysis Week

February
African American History Month
Library Lovers Month
National Cherry Month
National Weddings Month
Potato Lovers Month

February by the Week
First Week – Women's Heart Week
Second Week – National Crime Prevention Week
Third Week – Pay Your Bills Week
Fourth Week – Read Me Week

March
Academy Awards Month
National Craft Month
National Noodle Month
National Peanut Month
Women's History Month

March by the Week
First Week – Return Borrowed Books Week
Second Week – Brain Awareness Week
Third Week – National Manufacturing Week
Fourth Week – American Chocolate Week

April
International Guitar Month
Keep America Beautiful Month
Listening Awareness Month
National Poetry Month
Stress Awareness

April by the Week
First Week – Golden Rule Week
Second Week – National Garden Week
Third Week – National Park Week
Fourth Week – National Lingerie Week

May
Asian Pacific American Heritage Month
Better Sleep Month
Mental Health Month
National Comfort Month
National Photo Month

May by the Week
First Week – National Postcard Week
Second Week – National Nurses Week
Third Week – National Bike Week
Fourth Week – National Backyard Games Week

June
Effective Communications Month
National Iced Tea Month
National Rose Month
Safety Month
Zoo and Aquarium Month

June by the Week
First Week – National Fragrance Week
Second Week – Meet a Mate Week
Third Week – Lightning Safety Awareness Week
Fourth Week – Fish are Friends, Not Food Week

July
Anti Boredom Month
Blueberries Month
Fireworks Safety Month
Ice Cream Month
International Blondie and Deborah Harry Month

July by the Week
First Week – Be Nice to New Jersey Week
Second Week – Nude Recreation Weekend
Third Week – Coral Reef Awareness Week
Fourth Week – Open week – start your own special week

August
Family Meal Month
Foot Health Month
Happiness Happens Month
National Golf Month
National Inventor's Month

August by the Week
First Week – Clown Week
Second Week – Elvis Week
Third Week – National Friendship Week
Fourth Week – Be Kind to Humankind Week

September
Classical Music Month
Latino Heritage Month
National Honey Month
Pleasure Your Mate Month
Shameless Promotion Month

September by the Week
First Week – International Enthusiasm Week
Second Week – Bald is Beautiful Days
Third Week – Tolkien Week
Fourth Week – Constitution Week

October
Clergy Appreciation Month
Country Music Month
German-American Heritage Month
Positive Attitude Month
Quality Month

October by the Week
First Week – World Space Week
Second Week – Fire Prevention Week
Third Week – National Character Counts Week
Fourth Week – Peace, Friendship, and Goodwill Week

November
American Indian Heritage Month
I Am So Thankful Month
International Drum Month
National Novel Writing Month (NaNoWriMo)
World Communication Month

November by the Week
First Week – National Fig Week
Second Week – World Kindness Week
Third Week – American Education Week
Fourth Week – Better Conversation Week

December
Bingo's Birthday Month
Safe Toys and Gifts Month
National Tie Month
Universal Human Rights Month
Spiritual Literacy Month

December by the Week
First Week – Cookie Cutter Week
Second Week – Human Rights Week
Third Week – International Language Week
Fourth Week – It's About Time Week

Appendix IV
Helpful Websites

Books and Games

www.EducationalLearningGames.com

www.christianbook.com

E-cards

www.bluemountain.com

www.myfuncards.com

www.regards.com

General Reference

www.brownielocks.com

www.printablechecklists.com

www.refdesk.com

Romance

www.1001waystoberomantic.com

Appendix V
Month and Anniversary Gift Information

Anniversary	Traditional	Modern
1	Paper	Clocks
2	Cotton	China
3	Leather	Crystal, Glass
4	Linen (Silk)	Appliances
5	Wood	Silverware
6	Iron	Wood objects
7	Wool (Copper)	Desk sets
8	Bronze	Linens, lace
9	Pottery (China)	Leather goods
10	Tin, Aluminum	Diamond
11	Steel	Fashion Jewelry
12	Silk	Pearls, Colored Gems
13	Lace	Textiles, Furs
14	Ivory	Gold jewelry
15	Crystal	Watches
16		Silver hollowware
17		Furniture
18		Porcelain
19		Bronze
20	China	Platinum
21		Brass, nickel
22		Copper
23		Silver plate
24		Musical Instruments
25	Silver	Sterling silver
26		Original pictures
27		Sculpture
28		Orchids
29		New furniture
30	Pearl	Diamond

Anniversary	Traditional	Modern
31		Timepieces
32		Conveyances (e.g. car)
33		Amethyst
34		Opal
35	Coral (Jade)	Jade
36		Bone china
37		Alabaster
38		Beryl, Tourmaline
39		Lace
40	Ruby	Ruby
41		Land
42		Improved real estate
43		Travel
44		Groceries
45	Sapphire	Sapphire
46		Original poetry tribute
47		Books
48		Optical goods (e.g. telescope, microscope)
49		Luxuries, any kind
50	Gold	Gold

Appendix VI
Favorites

Actor (living)	
Actor (of all time)	
Actress (living)	
Actress (of all time)	
Aerobic Activity	
Album / CD	
Animal	
Aroma	
Artist	
Athlete	
Author	
Ballad	
Baseball Team	
Basketball Team	
Beer	
Bible Passage	
Board Game	
Body part (Spouse's)	
Body part (Yours)	
Book (fiction)	
Book (Non-fiction)	
Brand of make-up	
Bread	
Breed of cat	
Breed of dog	
Broadway play	
Candy	
Car (make & year)	
Champagne	
Children's Book	
City	
Classical composer	
Coffee	

Favorites Continued	
Cologne / After shave	
Color	
Color for Car	
Comedian	
Comfort food	
Comic character	
Comic strip	
Cookie	
Country Song	
Dance Tune	
Day of the Week	
Designer	
Dessert	
Drink	
Erotic clothing (for spouse)	
Erotic clothing (for self)	
Fabric to wear	
Fairy tale	
Fast Food Joint	
Fictional Character	
Flower	
Food	
Football Team	
Foreign country	
Foreplay activity (to perform)	
Foreplay activity (to receive)	
Fruit	
Gemstone	
Gift ever received	
Gospel Song	
Hairstyle	
Hero	

Favorites Continued	
Heroine	
Historical Personality	
Hobby	
Holiday	
Ice cream	
Ice cream toppings	
Indoor Activity	
Jazz number	
Jewelry metal	
Kind of Chocolate	
Leisure activity	
Literary genre	
Magazine	
Massage type	
Meal	
Month of the Year	
Movie	
Movie genre	
Movie: action	
Movie: adventure	
Movie: comedy	
Movie: erotic	
Movie: romantic comedy	
Museum	
Music genre	
Music Group	
Music to make love to	
Musical	
Olympic Sport	
Opera	
Outdoor Activity	
Painting	
Pastry	
Perfume	

Favorites Continued	
Photographer	
Pizza toppings	
Place to be touched erotically	
Poem	
Poet	
Precious metal	
Proverb	
R&B tune	
Restaurant (expensive)	
Restaurant (frugal)	
Rock 'n Roll Song	
Role model (actual person)	
Role model (fictional)	
Romantic Song	
Room in your home	
Saying	
Scent	
Sculpture	
Season of the year	
Sex atmosphere	
Sex place	
Sex time	
Sexual activity	
Sexual position	
Sexy outfit (for spouse)	
Sexy outfit (for self)	
Show tune	
Singer	
Slow Dance Song	
Snack	
Soda	
Song	

Favorites Continued	
Songwriter	
Sport	
Sport (to play)	
Sport (to watch)	
Store	
Style of artwork	
Style of clothing (for spouse)	
Style of clothing (for self)	
Symphony	
Television show (current)	
Television show (old)	
Time of Day	
Touch	
TV cartoon	
TV cartoon character	
TV drama	
TV sitcom	
Type of exercise	
Type of jewelry	
Vacation activity	
Vacation place	
Vegetable	
Vehicle	
Way to get energized	
Way to relax	
Way to spend lazy afternoon	
Wine	
Workout	

Appendix VII
Recommended Reading

Chapman, Gary. *The Five Love Languages.* Chicago: Northfield Publishing, 1995.

Godek, Gregory J.P. *1001 Ways To Be Romantic.* Naperville, Illinois: Sourcebooks, Inc., 2000.

Godek, Gregory J.P. *10,000 ways to say i love you.* Naperville, Illinois: Sourcebooks, Inc., 1999.

Gottman, John and Nan Silver. *The Seven Principles for Making Marriage Work.* New York: Three Rivers Press, 1999.

Harley, Willard F., Jr. *His Needs Her Needs.* Grand Rapids: Fleming H. Revell, 1986.

Harley, Willard F., Jr. *5 Steps To Romantic Love.* Grand Rapids: Fleming H. Revell, 1993.

Haynes, Cyndi and Dale Edwards. *2002 Questions and Answers for Lovers.* Avon, Massachusetts: Adams Media Corporation, 2000.

Haynes, Cyndi and Dale Edwards. *2002 Things To Do On A Date.* Avon, Massachusetts: Adams Media Corporation, 1999.

Haynes, Cyndi and Dale Edwards. *2002 Romantic Ideas.* Avon, Massachusetts: Adams Media Corporation, 1998.

For additional recommended books and other resources go to the resources page at www.myrealmarriage.com.

Printed in the United States
78558LV00003B/1-132